A Prism of Poetry

Michael S. Lopez

Copyright © 2019 Michael S. Lopez

All rights reserved.

ISBN-10: 1091823529
ISBN-13: 978-1091823525

DEDICATION

To my Mom and Dad, thank you for being patient and giving me the freedom to explore.

To Dean, thank you for being supportive and understanding.

To my friends, my extended family, thank you for being there, encouraging me, and making me laugh.

To my early critics from my writing circle, Carol, Lori, Marti, Kevin, and Tonya, thank you for making me think, stretch, and edit.

About the Poetry

These poems span my lifetime, from my teenage years until now. This venture has been cathartic, writing about the joys, the loves, the sadness, and the pain of my life. I have my muses who have truly inspired me, and continue to do so. I share some of my loves and losses. I expose some of my dark thoughts and times. I recall and offer life lessons, either by experiencing them or teaching them. Lastly, I end with some silliness and humor. I do hope you enjoy the journey.

Warning

There are mild obscenities within.

There are some dark thoughts.

About Me

I am a teacher.

I am a husband.

I am a best friend.

I am a student.

I am an Air Force brat.

I am a brother.

I am a son.

I am curious.

I am motastic.

I observe.

I learn.

I dream.

I help.

I inspire.

I care.

I bleed.

I am not a label.

I am more.

More About Me

I was born in Hawaii. I grew up an Air Force brat and traveled half the globe. I interacted with different people and cultures for the first twelve years of my life. I found this awe-inspiring and fascinating. It was from these experiences that my love of learning and for exploration grew. I have earned a bachelor's degree in psychology, a teaching credential, and a master's degree in education. Currently, I live in Northern California.

Intro

Prism

What is clear
Maybe not be simple
Take a different perspective
And change the outcome

What starts as absent
Becomes a rainbow
One holds many
Colorful, daring, and bright

Each needs to discover
Their own frequency
You are not alone
In this unwavering boldness

Unleash your power
Shine your own light
No longer be the prism
Be a leader of the enlightenment

Creation

I have always known
I have wanted to create
Reading fueled the imagination
Taking me to new heights

The words I assimilated
Shine and sparkle
They are odd shaped pieces
Eager to please and transform

I lay them all out
Like a mysterious puzzle
I look for the bigger picture
To hone my attention and speak to me

I start with the ending
Then work backward to evolve
It is a strange process
With its wild ebb and flow

Truth be told
It is exciting not to know
Until the very end
When the brilliance itself shows

Hiding in Plain Sight

I am human
A male of my race
I bleed, and I feel
It is evident on my bad poker face

Childhood is less than desirable
Lots of disappointment and rain
The masks, walls, and lies begin
Welcome to my theater of pain

The teen years aren't much better
Knowing religion's doctrine
Facing a deadly epidemic
Experiencing society's odium

When I become a man
I begin to breathe fresh air
The freedom to explore me
And find what is really out there

I pick my way cautiously
For the past has taught me well
Trust has always been an issue
It is my personal living hell

The masks, walls, and lies serve their purpose
Maybe, possibly, all too well
Who am I
No one can really tell

If you dare
Walk the labyrinth and find your way
I hope you can understand
The reasons why I hid the truth about being gay

The Question

One of life's greatest mysteries
Is the complexity by which we are bound
Going by the same token
How does one define oneself
Better yet, who am I

Am I a familial genetic melting pot
Have I completed many past lives
Am I an alien experiment
Has God predestined my life's course
Where do I start

What grounds do I base my beliefs on
How am I going to discover my identity
Confusion and doubt fog my perceptions
Misinformation and good intentions muddy the truth
My head spins

What has been plastered, spoken, or printed
Intrudes and dominates the narrative
Little bright screens
Illuminate, titillate, and influence
So much bombardment

Am I a sum of my parts
Do I project a different me
If I look in a mirror
Is that what I am
Is this the mystery to be solved

No, I have it all wrong
So much to filter and synthesize
To accept or reject
It is not the question of who I am
It is the simple truth of who I was

Bold

I am the type of person
That is passionate
Demanding
Loyal

Time is too short
For anything less
I want to see you
The true you

I bond that way
Through honesty
Respect
Caring

Am I perfect
Hell no
I do come armed with
A warning label

I hold nothing back
Wanting only the best
I am worth it
I am bold

Muses

Sighted

I have seen the world
In shades of gray
Hollow searching wisps

Certain types of blindness
Are this way
Especially that of the heart

Until I met you
I could only dream of
What color is

Your blue eyes sparkled
When our eyes connected
I saw them, I saw you

To this day, after so many years
You are all the color
I have ever needed to see

Blue

Certainty counters the what ifs
While wisdom banishes the lies
Rejection becomes the truth
As hope continues to torture

It is not fair
This you and me
It just is
This abnormal love whatever

I have buried the feelings
I have sot counseling
I have even stayed away
The solutions are just as torturous

So here I am
A puppet swinging by its complicated strings
Built on so many years
Laced by so many beautiful memories

What the heart wants
Hurts so bloody badly
I thought you should know
Always

The Love Inside

The love I feel
Comes from deep inside
It is a faith
That needs no guide

A love so selfless
It basks in all your splendor
My heart has never known
Such a beautiful wonder

My love is real
Given freely to you
Such an easy thing
So deep, so true

Know what is here
Inside my beating heart
Is so passionate and pure
Ever for you, will it part

The Key to My Heart

Do you know
You have a key to my heart
Though this was not planned
I would not have it any other way

I was surprised by this
After so many years together
You persist so strongly
I just surrender to the thoughts and dreams of you

I must tell you
I love you more
With each passing day
You resonate deep within my soul

Should I tell you
Of what has been done
Can there be hope
To what has been given

Do you know …

The Draw

When I think about love
I think of one person
The connection is so powerful
It is chemistry, electricity

I feel all aflutter
I float
I do the goo goo eyes
I am definitely not in control

My heart pounds
Sometimes skipping a beat
I want to pound on my chest
It is that carnal

I see the ruggedness
I know the tenderness
What can I say
You do it for me

I thought you should know
Truth be told
When you are ready
I am here

The Caveman

I really noticed you one particular Halloween
Truth be told, it was your costume
That low-cut revealing caveman onesie
Which hung over one shoulder and barely over your ass

Body hair jutted everywhere
Adding to your rugged masculinity
Excited baby blues danced
As your daring machismo flirted

I knew I was in trouble
More so, after I caught your husky scent
I tried to resist that and watching you strut
Soon, I started studying every inch of your body

I barely knew you then
But I knew I wanted to know more
Butterflies fluttered and heart pounding
I dared myself to try

I bumped into you, accidently
You smiled and steadied me in our first dance
Good Lord, I thought
Who's the caveman now

Risk

Religious persecution
The outbreak of AIDS
Getting disowned, thrown out
Being beaten, killed

I had my concerns
But I made my decision
Not to act and lie anymore
I opened the closet and exited

I was so terrified
To let you know my secret
I gambled and bet on you
For good measure, I hoped and prayed too

Will you understand
Will you accept me
Will you still be my best friend
I began to shake

Tears welled
I started and stopped three times
Show your pride
Take the risk

I made it to your door
Wiping away the tears
I slowed my breathing
Only one brave knock needed

You answered, almost knowing
I bore my true self
All the while searching your face
I started to cry

You pulled me close
Hugging me tight
You whispered in my ear
"We will be alright"

Moments of You

I sneak around
When you least expect
Stealing snippets here and there
Never being suspect

I relish in my audacity
Being a clever little thief
I am charming yet daring
Well, that is my smug belief

But then, the tables are turned
When I am drawn into your light
I am not able to resist
How can this be right

The thief is not me
As the realization becomes scary
Past heartbreaks resurface
And I become flighty and weary

But it is too late
I am trapped in your strong arms
I panic and try to resist
Your devilish intoxicating charms

I blame my impulsive need
To possess the best parts of you
Am I dope to believe
That this dream can actually come true

Time seems to stop
As I face the costs of my foolish foray
The obvious moment of truth
It is you who steals me away

The Forbidden

It all starts with that chance meeting
I knew then I was in trouble
Reason flew right out the window
A lustful temptation eagerly saluted

I needed to know
Was it a reality, or a fantasy
Unfortunately, unjust reality won out
And hopes were dashed

Come to find out however
They weren't extinguished
Thus, my current continuing dilemma
Friendship, or pleasure

It has been torture, all these years
The dreams and the drunken closeness
They severely blur the line
Damnit, what am I to do

I relish in your hug
I know your scent
Hell, I've seen you naked
Now I know your kiss

This doesn't quell the passion
It makes it an inferno
Why does the forbidden
Feel so right in every way

One fleeting thought of you
Becomes two
Then more, then even more
This adds to the confusion, the yearning

You're my breath
My Adonis
My kryptonite
My best friend

Damn it …

Love Walked In

When I was younger
I thought I had a grasp on that emotion
But one moment changes everything
Mine was that day
You walked into my life

Was it that cocky arrogance
That gigolo swagger
That peeking chest hair
Those soulful baby blues
Hell, it was the entire package

The connection was electric
Daring and hungry
I just fell, so hard
I knew you were the one
That one, the soulmate kind

The bond grew stronger
Innocence transmuted into yearning
Lines became blurry
Then finally, they intersected
Boom, fireworks

It is funny
The random thoughts
That come full circle
Being made complete
Made whole

Even after all these years
I am still reminded of
Every time I see you
The day love walked in
And stayed

Time with You

I find you working on an old car
Tired, sweaty, and grumbling
Perfect, good thing I stopped by
On the other hand, I do get a great view

I try not to stare, but come on
While you're on your back half way under
You somehow know and bust me
"Are you enjoying the view"

"What, what are you talking about"
"Sure, right"
He does a slow Sharon Stone
Shit now, I know the color of his bikini briefs

Okay, I'm at midsalute
Damn him to hell
"I know you're smiling under there"
"Am not, okay, a lot"

It is this game we play
Always on his terms
He crawls out and shifts positions
Oh lord, now he's on all fours

He asks for a socket something
My eyes were transfixed
I hand him the wrong tool
"Ha, you feed my ego"

Oh sorry, but so not sorry
He works, we talk
I help, drool, and fantasize
It is time well spent

Intervention

There are times
When you go away
I do not mean far
I mean from being here, present

You go through the motions
Light and half-hearted
Your spark has been diminished
A darkness is seeping in

I care too much
To sit idly by
I try to intervene, help
Since one-word answers come my way

How to approach
Kind touch, or heavy handed
I make contact, face-to-face
You resist, still fronting

I relent
Bear-hugging you fiercely
You break
Letting it out, letting me in

Human contact
Is a great cure all
It wonders and amazes
It comforts and heals

It is quiet for a while
So I wait
Your spark reignites
It is a start
You are not alone
Ever

Constant

You have help nurture
Hope out of ashes
You have shown me
How to live again
It is a treasured gift

I know I joke
That you are my backup husband
It is because I have never known
Such endless love and support
Like what I receive from you

You are there for me
Even when it is the little things
You listen, you hug, you cry
I can't imagine how I got so lucky
You make me a better man

I have healed and grown stronger
Nourished and enlightened
You sometimes ask why the hugs are longer
The texts random, the calls deep
I am returning what I was taught

It is authentic passionate love
From the best part of my life
The person who has always been there
My constant

In My Life

It is that first chance meeting
That grabs your attention
It is like wow, be still my heart
I am in, I want to know more

You are awkward yet daring
Making a connection
Magnetic, electric
It is when words fail, hearts skip

It is when actions must speak
Hope rises, courage blazes
You do this to me
You make me want, you

God, I could easily fall
So hard, so fast
I am drawn in
Captured openly, eagerly

I look back at our beginning
After so many years and such great memories
I know how blessed I am
With you in my life

Date Night

Under a star-filled sky
Soft music accompanies a blazing firepit
Excellent bourdon flows freely
It is a good start to "date" night

Okay, so you wouldn't call it that
Being straight and married and all
But it is very rare indeed
That we get this alone time

No "wives," no kids
Crude jokes and pigginess fly
It is such a relaxing natural ease
Sharing and being here with you

So many years have passed
So much reminiscing is had
It is like a good comfortable marriage
All loving and strong

You hate it when I do that
"Rainbowing" it all up
Don't you know by now, bestie
I love it when we kiss and make up

The Bond

When I called you that day
I never suspected
The dire straights
Until I heard that crack in your voice

I have never heard you that scared
Mr. Fix-it was dumbfounded, broken
I wanted to drive over to be there
I wanted to fiercely bear hug you

Since I couldn't do that at this moment
I shut the hell up and listened
I empathized and encouraged
I was what you needed, a friend

You got it all out
You evened your breathing
I knew you were in control
You had a plan, ready for action

An hour had passed
But neither of us noticed
Being "here" was all that mattered
It speaks to that connection, our bond

Sweet Nothings

It began innocently enough
Over emails and phone calls
You made me so happy
That I was bouncing off the walls

Your sweet Southern charm
Captured my broken heart
The hope for love was restored
I was being given a fresh start

So, day after day
We built a foundation
That spanned 3000 miles
Made of promises and devotion

I think of you often
So much so
That my silly smile hurts
And I begin to glow

You have marked my life
Down to the very core of my soul
You mean the world to me
For you have made me whole

The Simple Joys

It is all too easy
To think of you
You are so pronounced in my mind
That even random thoughts
Have a touch of you

It is a simple joy
That warms my heart
It is like hearing that reverberation
Of your sensual Southern drawl
With its rugged tenderness

Understand
I do not regret
Or even complain
I just cherish what I have
Though it is but a piece of you
It is enough

It is a foundation
For a future
That is built
One day at a time
With hope and faith as guides

The Dream

It starts the same
You calling me that pet name
I track your voice
But the fog is foreboding and dense

Searching for you becomes intense
So I wait for you to appear
My spoken name comes again
Dripping with lust and promise

Then you are next to me
Breathing in my ear
In that sexy Southern voice
Making it an easy choice to fall

You caress me with tempting words
Then your exploring fingers follow
I shiver and gasp
You make me soar
Oh God

I grasp for you
But you are not here
I panic
No, it's too soon
Please stay

You reappear
Hopes arise anew
Passion erupts
Eventually, you steal a piece of me
With a long zealous kiss

Then you are gone
Like you are not even there
But your scent lingers
As does the taste of your lips

I hate it now
As this futile reality stirs
I must let this go
This heavy weight on my heart

I will wait
Loving by grace
Yearning and resolute
For you are worth it

Southern Comfort

It is like a warm hand-me-down quilt
On a lazy Sunday morning
Which dares to kiss and caress
Promising more than a mere beginning

Memories begin to flow then
Adding slowly to the welcoming
A content smirk form wryly
Reassuring the blissful reminiscing

It is a dream-like state of ecstasy
Which starts the raw awakening
I must comply, never deny
The feelings that are strengthening

That is how it is
When I think of you
If I never told you before
Consider this something new, yet true

The Fire

After the initial spark
I bathe in the wanton desire
Fate has played her part
Fanning the flames of this newly found fire

I am consumed by the calling heat
And the pull of the hypnotic dancing lights
I become a new source of fuel
For the passion of this night

I rise and fall with the roaring blaze
Equally flaring with erotic precision
The rapture is so intense
I could never have fathomed or envisioned

So after a time of just burning
This gratifying fervor subsides
The memory will always linger
Where it belongs, deep inside

Intoxicating Euphoria

In the stillness of a moment
I just fell away
Though in your strong arms
I did not go far

It was an intoxicating euphoria
That assaulted my senses
All my defenses crumbled
I was at your loving mercy

With passing heartbeats
You whispered such sweet murmurs
Though I tingled to my soul's core
I just laid next to you and relished

Really nothing needed to be said
It was one perfect night
One innocent evening
Floating

Here at Night

In the waning of the moonlight
Peeping through the curtain's sheen
Spying and witnessing a beginning
The moon's glow matches my own

It is another night
In the warmth and comfort of your bed
I watch you sleep soundly
Until you roll over and grab for me

I smile sheepishly
Though you do not see
This makes me so happy
Having you here naked with me

The moon shies away
Having a satisfying answer
I eagerly cuddle with you
Adding a long tender kiss
And much, much more

Red

I took a chance
Letting my heart hope
One more time
Though it is never easy
That is what faith is for
I jumped

I took my time however
Going slow
Heart on my sleeve
Honesty to a fault
You needed to see
This is me
Warts and all

So you are proof
That wishes do come true
All I had to do was believe
And I so did
Now all I see
Is nothing but red

Love

The Stalker

I am relaxing in my garden
When a neighboring cat strolled by
Something caught its eye
A-hunting it does go

I am transfixed by this sauntering
Weaving through the shadows
It is a lot like a tango
Bold and seductive

It is a blissful ignorance
Until you know something's wrong
You are dazed and confused
Horrified and excited

Bam, then you are caught
In its fiendish tender grasp
Your heart pounds
You get flushed

Before you are consumed
The fever pitch explodes
It is all over now
Welcome to love

If ...

If you let me in
Then you would have someone to hold onto
Consider the possibilities
No longer one, but two

If I am given a chance
Then I would surely take that fall
I would be downed by a blessed angel
The most heavenly one of all

If you give into doubt or fear
Then we will never be
I trust you wholeheartedly
Please believe in a you and me

If you know what is in your heart
Then dare to set that love free
I will be there to support you
Or help you up from that fall to your knees

If this is to be
Then my hopes and dreams would come true
You would become my breath of life
All because love pointed me to you

Acrobat

I don my costume and mask
For it is almost time to perform
Life in the circus of misfits and oddities
I have never felt so comfortable
Home is definitely where the heart is

I prepare my mindset
By organizing my priorities
Inside everyone hides one desire
Though they often feel
Outside no one would know or care

Luckily, we are a hearty breed
Trained to defy
To conquer the fear of failure
We climb to new heights courage
With no time to hesitate or second guess

Creativity fuels a fire
Equal to what's inside
Danger is also there
Closer to the edge

I fly solo without a safety net
I trust the catcher will be there
Is it safer to hang on
Or is it safer to let go

I outstretch my hands, my faith
As this act unfolds
Time won't slip away
For this time, I grab my chance

A Little Reminder

You feel you cannot do this
However, I know better
You are not alone
You must know this

I know it is all wrong
What happened back then
But it is still here
Haunting and eroding

You feel full of darkness
Alone, helpless, and lost
It is only a passing thing
This heaviness drowning you from within

You must know
This darkness will pass
Another day will come
Hope will be your guide

You thought of turning back
Only you did not
Though you did not feel it then
You are stronger than you know

You kept going
Not knowing totally why
You know what I speak of
That drive to stay alive

Why do I remind you
Of all that once was
Because sometimes show
Is better than tell

The Test

Fighting the fear and doubt within
For the reason that he only knows
The candle is constantly flickering
He is trying to let his feelings show

Dare he take that chance
Knowing that his whole ego could crumble
He steps with his right foot forward
Being very hopeful and extremely humble

A tear runs down his cheek
Seemingly from a dry yet determined eye
His arms open without question
Because without him he would rather die

The practiced daydream dispenses
As does a deep longing sigh
It is time for the real thing
There is no greater reward without a true try

However, rejection on so many levels is a factor
Being outed, being gay
In this time of the 80's
This can be a foolish and deadly foray

He approaches the man of his dreams
Adrenalin pumping courage, the leading emotion
He grabs his attention, being quite forward
Finally popping the burning question

Flight Attendant

I have learned to fly again
And it is because of you
You have nurtured my damaged wings
Are you my dream come true

It is hard for me to trust
As you found out
And why I did for you
Is still a mighty mystery

I let you in
And I have been blessed ever since
When you spoke those words
Every doubt left its iron hold

You were patient and encouraging
You took sweet loving care
I did not know what to say
For no one has loved me like that

So here we are
On this ledge of life's grand adventure
I am terrified to try this again
But at least, I am not alone

The Candle

And so, it begins
Sprinkle, sprinkle, splash
Rap, rap, tap
Rumble, rumble, flash

The wind howls against the storm's rage
I feel the coldness of their argument
Through the misty battered window
I shudder as the thunder roars

While I endure this lonely night
I recall your soft longing touch
As you lit my fire
I joyfully burn for you
For you know, you own my heart

I stand tall on this window's ledge
Braving the darkness that surrounds me
I sit, I wait, I cry
I would like to shrivel up for my faults
And eventually, I do

The tears of missing you
Burn as they stream downward
Am I brave at heart
Or foolish at heart
That is the one true question

Though I never tire in my duties for you
I sometimes flicker ever so
At times, I feel like
My brilliance goods unnoticed
Alas, I am wrong

From out of the cold wet gloom
I hear the click of the front door lock
I am not alone
I burn brighter

I feel silly doubting
Entertaining that stupid uncertainty
The lights come on
And you are revealed

You are that special someone
Who always takes the time
To give me that sweet gentle kiss
Which satisfies my fire
And shows me that you truly care

Metamorphosis

After I left the protectorate of the nest
I used my small uncomplicated form
To creep into this strange new world
I followed the instincts of my heart

Danger lurked everywhere
I saw it in a flying shadow
I heard it on whispering winds
I felt it in the rumbling earth

Still, the ache in my wanting heart
Urged me forward
I searched cautiously
Dreaming and hoping carefree

Time became my trusty companion
While I clawed and crawled my way
Then, suddenly, you appear
Seemingly out of thin air

You sauntered toward me
Sweeping me off my feet
Our first dance
Eyes starry and daring

My heart fluttered madly
As I began to absorb your aura
You pulsed and radiated
Reaching my guarded lonely soul

Once my closest companion
Time betrayed my trust
Forcing our relationship to change
Ripping us apart

At first, it was you
Then, I felt the strain
Being cocooned within our worlds
Words couldn't express the pain

All of a sudden
It got quiet, sullen
I went numb, empty
Depleted by careless whispers

Depression gave into recollection
Transformation blossomed and flourished
I had changed into someone new
I was no longer bound

I was free to fly
Able to search for the right love
My outlook became much brighter
For love had made me

Our Song

I lay next to you in bed
Reveling in how lucky I am
That you choose me
Day after day
Year after year

I just can't help myself
Listening to your heartbeat
It lifts me, sustains me
This is my happy
Our life together

There is no doubt
You are my world
My reason to shine
My reason to fall
In love, again and again

As I hold you
I acknowledge this inspired tribute
Our heartbeats in unison
Our song
And knowing what complete is

What Love Is

Fate has crossed our paths
So we could meet
I was being given a chance
To open up my heart

When I saw you
For the first time
I held my breath
And I dared to hope

I summoned up the courage
For a fumbled introduction
That did not matter though
For your eyes mirrored mine

That memory flashes now
For it is our anniversary
Though many years have passed
The feeling remains intensely the same

I still hold my breath
Every time I see you
For I am reminded of
What love is

Home

The happiest moments of joy
Involve the closeness of friends and family
They make the experience better
Sharing in the love of the moment

It is always time well spent
The conversations, the hugs, the pictures,
The inclusion, the acceptance
No need to hide, or pretend, just be

I cherish what is
It is special and right
Warm fuzzies abound
All throughout night

Sometimes, it is too much
Way over the top
Such is the way of life
Especially with so many memorable characters

Appreciate and enjoy what you have
The extensions of your world
It is true with what is said
Home is where the heart is

Roots

The magical day arrives
It is a choice, a commitment
The day two becomes one

Lust and love have bonded
Entangled, rooted
This newness, this together

A grand adventure awaits
Being explored, shared
Nurtured, loved

The support cultivates growth
A solid unity
It reaches out, it spreads

A family sprouts
Reflections of the same
Happiness, loveliness

This attracts new varieties
Gathering, coming together
Becoming a devoted community

It is special kind of closeness
Blood-born, friendship-born
This is my family

Love Hurts

One

I am the only one
Left on mother tree
I desire to be like everyone else
Freed from the chains that bind me

At times, the wind comes and dances with me
And like always, I shudder at the first touch
Awakened are the buried passions
Which I have denied so much

The gentle kiss of the wind
Arouses my hungry lonely soul
I grasp for the solidarity
But alas, I cannot take hold

The sweet loving caress
Is but a fleeting and hollow affair
Suddenly, the wind moves on
And I am left with dead air

I become plagued and distressed
By the emptiness of the need
There has to be more than
The bold arrogance of the wind's misdeed

So I am deflated again
In my search of complete rapture
My teary eyes still survey for
The moment I become captured

Takes Two

This comfortable lull bothers me
The daily routines have become automatic
I don't know where your heart is
Why won't you show me

This is why love hurts, our love
I know what we have is real
I need you to help us
Talk, and talk from the heart

I am right here, always
Please reach out and show me
I don't want to be still anymore
I want us to be fulfilled again

Take the first step
Show me I am worth it
Let the vows remind you
Say love

Toss the Coin

Can a leopard change its spots
The spots that dot the past
So large, so true
Yet the claim is
That of change

Do you trust again
Knowing what can happen
Flesh for breakfast
Blood for lunch
Heart for dinner
How much is enough

Another fight
Another tear
Do you stay
Or do you go
The mind says yes
The heart says no

Emotions pull at you
Demanding an audience
The love, the memories
Is it time to be selfish
And stand on your own
Is it time to say when
Is it time to be alone

Weakness

I am at your door again
Praying for your audience
Desire drives me here
Please take me into your den of darkness

I crave your fierce caress
That passionate madness
It is almost vampiric
I volunteer to be your favorite innocence

You open the front door with a mischievous grin
Sweet everythings lure me in
You lead me into your bedroom
The lust is palpable

I stop, heart pounding
My knees buckle
I suck in my breath, hesitating
Your adventurous tongue breaks my indecision

Our animalistic passion
Cause flames to erupt
It is a runaway conflagration
It is raw and animalistic

Desire fuels, then consumes
It is all about this moment
Our erotic appetites
The veracity craves that I have more

Soon, I equal your voracity
I surprise you
I take control
You need to please me

It is ironic
After this spectacular night is over
It is you
Who begs me to stay

Pieces of You

You are gone now
But there is so much of you
Left behind
Pieces everywhere

No matter where I look
All I feel is this pain
My heart is shattered
The loneliness is crippling

I think of you
All the time
It hurts so much
Tears rain out of me

I can't sleep
I can't eat
You are the best part of me
My whole reason

I ache
I am lost and alone
Plagued by memorable snippets
Love shouldn't be like this

Breaking Point

I am being interrogated again
The questions are as sharp as knives
Jealousy tends to do this
I dread the fight that is on the horizon

This is our vicious little love circle
One shred of doubt strikes the match
Lots of insecurity adds the kindling
Then the conflagration blossoms

I cannot take much more of this
I have tried to be understanding and flexible
I am like a palm tree in a hurricane
Is this love worth the grief

This is how I am
If change will come
Then I am the one to change
I am the priority, worth it

I remember what is like to be alone
I know what it is like to be with him
I will not lose myself here
Though I question if this is the right decision

Am I being too rational
Am I being too reactionary
The trail of tears helps me decide
It is time to … just walk away

Heartache

You get lost in the pain
Not knowing which way is up, out
It hurts so damn much
The fetal position is of little comfort

Anger flares and rears its ugliness
Hitting something is the only solution
You want something to feel like you do
You punch again and again until you are all spent

Tears pour, bearing your sorrow
They threaten to consume you, drown you
Their undertow eventually takes you under
The weight is so heavy, unbearable

You break the surface
Gasping for air, freedom
Still fighting for something
Grasping for something solid, real

Darkness greets you instead
Swallowing you whole
You are tired, you surrender
You sink, letting go

A jolt shocks you
A lifeline emerges
You find the strength
You hang on, you go on

Sleep finds you, food does not
Another day comes, then a string more
The desolation ebbs
Walking dead seems right

Time helps close the wound
Distance helps patch the scar
Getting older instills wisdom, clarity
It is a process, heartache

Damned

A tear falls
Burning a trail down my cheek
Why can't it be that yesterday
When I met you that week

I cast the tear away
Like sand into the sea
Wishing for a different ending
Not this existing futility

We loved carefree
Unknowing the sands of time tick
Then out of the blue
You became horribly sick

I tried to be strong
And be by your side
I was weak and could not
I decided to run and hide

I ran so far away
Leaving you all terribly alone
Only my needs fueled me
While chills of death echoed to the bone

I didn't come back
On the day that you died
I contemplated returning
But I never even tried

So here I am now
Talking to a tombstone
Asking for forgiveness that I don't deserve
Trying to feel with my heart of stone

I get no response
As it begins to rain
I embrace God's tears
Wishing they will wash away the pain

I join in the concert of tears
Hoping to drown in my sorrow
I am such a coward
How can I face another tomorrow

I made a solemn vow
As I knelt in this wet gloom
The next person who comes along
My heart will have to make room

I leave your gravesite
Pulling myself out of this crushing despair
It is time to move on
Damned to finally know what it is like to truly care

Tortured

It was all just a dream
But was it really all in my head
When I look back now
All I see is me falling for you

It does not really matter
It is all over now
Then why do I feel so torn
I cannot brush this aside and move on

It still seems so real
You are all I have ever wanted
I am not in control
Why can't I let this go

There's nothing more to say
So it really does not matter
I shouldn't want you now
But I still do

Strong Enough

The last of the tears have hit the floor
I refuse to cry for you anymore
You are not worthy of my love
I will take inspiration for high above

I cannot forgive you for the shredding of my heart
It was more important to you that we be apart
Issues disguised as excuses shows your cowardice
You were not man enough to simply address

I took my battered bleeding heart and walked away
Love was not my companion that day
It was hard to abandon that life and start anew
What happened to my dream come true

I know what I did was right
Some battles you are only meant to fight
You are reduced to a bad chapter
Which was burned with such well-deserved rapture

I continue on and thrive
I have rediscovered what it is to be alive
Though hurt and pain can be rough
I have discovered I am strong enough

Made of Glass

There it stood
In the store
On a high shelf
The perfect symbol
A little glass sailboat

Later that day
I gave it to him
And told him why
He cried with joy
It does represent us

We would sail someday
Just you and I
Happy we were
Until that first storm
Shipwrecking and dry-docking the dream

Many storms later
The love was gone
Disgust took its place
I was asked to go
Only tears accompanied me

Months later he grew careless
The sailboat fell of the dresser
It shattered into glass pieces
He just stared at the once-love
At the ruined dream

Darkness

Tainted

What happens when childhood has been violated
Where does that lost innocence go
What does take purity's place
The real question is
Do you really possess the heart to know

Rage, confusion, shame, and fear fill the void
Where goodness and trust once occupied
Love is transmuted into hate, then indifference
The gentle playful soul is tainted by crushing blackness

When an encounter occurs
With this fallen little angel
The situation usually is explosive or traumatic
Emotions tend to flare and be extremely chaotic

The cancer keeps eating away
Hour after hour and day after day
It is too much to handle and endure
You are scarred for life at a tender young age

The marrow that once was life
Has been poisoned and now decays
There is not much to look forward to
Save the constant broken promises
Falling to the bottom of your wishing well

Day by Day

Doesn't the struggle ever end
When do the rainbows and happy times come
Will there ever be a day
When I can truthfully say
That I am a part of it

Will you take my hand
And run with me
Through the wind and rain
Laughing and dancing
Happy and carefree

I will never stop trying
Even when darkness is near
Words are shallow
Actions are impolite
I stand and look nonetheless

Hope is there
Guiding me forward
Helping me up
Cheering me on
Daring me to try

I look for a day with joy
A rainbow without the pot of gold
I am willing to give all my love away
But when I reach out my hand
Why will no one take it

Disarm

The memory of it is real fuzzy
Mask
When this all began
Wall
Though it is connected with
Front
Hurt, frustration, disappointment, and pain;
Barrier
I have an issue with trust
Appearances
So this is why everyone is kept away
Obstacle
Even the closest to me
Conceal
For they could do the most damage
Rampart
And cause that accursed thundering rain;
Shield
Sometimes, I set myself up for falls
Hindrance
By believing in my self-made lies
Suppression
I get misled in the illusion of my so-called happiness
Barricade
And let insecurities whisper hope through my mind;
Protect
Cries of helplessness get drowned out and buried
Impediment
By the echoes and numerous empty corridors
Disguise

Of this maze that's been erected
Withhold
And to which I do not know how to get out of
Lost

Control

It is on a bad day like this
That I do not have enough strings
I am being pulled in various directions
Eventually, the strings snap
Releasing a multitude of unpleasant stings

I am a play thing
A child's well-loved puppet
With happiness painted on my face
It is not like a tic-tac-toe game
Where I can easily forfeit

A rough tug here
A violent pull there
My day is really flailing
When will someone respect me
And take gentle loving care

I am paraded around the room
Helpless and out of control
Equally thrashing and twirling about
I watch the show from the stage
Since I am the merry ole soul

When I am done with
Back to the cold dark closet I go
I force myself to continue on
Peeking through a keyhole
Often quoting, "On with the show"

What I see or feel
Does not really matter
Why do I know this
Because no one is asking
And I am the one hanging by strings

The Bind

Love becomes blind
Sometimes, deaf as well
After a while
Love and pain
Become one and the same

Compared to a drug
You need a fix
No matter the cost
No matter how desperate
Or vulnerable

You are stripped
Of principles
And value
You go against
Your better judgment

You fight a reality
Of what was
And what is
The truth is clear
Or it could be muddy

Because love and pain
Exist on the same coin
Do you take a chance
Being hopeful and brave
And flip it
Do you dare risk it
Is love worth it

The Edge

There is this point
On a ledge of this cliff
Where I often wonder
What would it be like to fly

I stare blankly
Until I remember why
Is it a decision of the weak
Or is it to stop a cycle of pain

There are gulls gliding
It looks so easy
A voice inside says
"Why don't you give it a try"

"This is madness"
Comes another voice
Such indecision and chaos
Will someone make up your mind

Dwelling on this
Brings only more painful sadness
Leave and come back
Have the courage for another day

I turn my back to the edge
And begin to walk away
This is the right choice
I just needed a running start
To fly

Husk

It is that time again
Where change and growth
Has taken its toll
And I am forced to comply

For when I see my distorted image
In the mirror of relentless vanity and deceit
I ponder and question if this is the right moment
And will this new journey be worth
The agony of transformation

My skin already commences to peel
Will the skin underneath be any better
Will I be pleased to be looked upon
Will this skin be the last

I rip, I tear, and I shred away
At the shell that I have portrayed
Why is it that every time I do this
I feel so exposed and hollow inside

I am a molting snake
As many as my lovers can attest to
I am looking for a better future
Or for the moment a more accurate costume

So out to the real world I go once more
Playing in the Marti-Gras of life
One thing is for certain though
If I do not like myself
I will husk further

Heartless

Love's fire burns white hot
The flames rage at both extremes
Bellowing smoke tears the eyes, clouding judgment
The darkness from within beams

Love's blanket wraps around to comfort
The heat causes some friction
The folds begin to tighten and smother
Protection from the cold—what a contradiction

Love's kiss tastes bittersweet
Especially when blood is drawn
Passion changes from fire to glass
Broken with the coming of the dawn

Love's bond links the heart to the soul
Chains reinforce the foundation
Instead of unity, you are caught
Trapped like a savage bottled emotion

When released from love's cruel grasp
The painful tears shred you apart
Black would be the color
If I still had a heart

Limitations

I know not the path
I should take
Each step forward
Is with monumental effort
Doubt, fear, and past pain
Hinders my fluid movement
My leg quivers
With each waking step
Am I alone in this
I question, looking around
But being the person I am
I do not ask for help
It is a cold comfort
That I am so used to
I revel in
My countless-ring circus
I take comfort
By the chaos it brings
I try one ring
For a while
However, the permanency
Frightens me off
To that safe place
Where the rings connect
Where I am not part of anything
The safest place to be
I cannot be disappointed
Or hurt
Of course
It is where
I do not belong

What is more frightening
The fact that
I am this way
The fact that
I am questioning change
The fact that
I don't know how to change

Abuse

Ring, ring, ring
The telephone is calling
I answer it eagerly
Only to find
Abuse on the other end

Instead of hanging up
I am captivated by the malevolence
The call could be considered obscene
If I was offended
By what I have heard

I am left exhilarated and bewildered
And I want more
I have been violated
In such an innocent way
That ecstasy has a new meaning

When I hang up
I question what I did
With the forbidden euphoria gone
And with higher reasoning returning
What did I do

The day goes by
As I race for an explanation
My mind is blank
Like a brand-new piece of paper
Maybe, that is the answer

I want to cross the line
Tired of being so vanilla
To the path less traveled
This is madness
Ring, ring, ring

I run to my choice unapologetically
Enthralled by a desperate need
I listen and prolong my suffering
But when the abuse ends
I cradle the phone
And I ask myself
Why do they keep calling me

Coin Sides

Loving and losing
Related kin
Change one letter
A huge degree of difference

Is it a friend
Is it an end
Sometimes swift
Sometimes prolonged

When there is a loss
The blow can be crippling
A hole is made
Where none existed

Mourning the finality
Crying and reminiscing
Acknowledging the void
No longer whole

Those who remain
Carry on in pieces
Togetherness helps softens
The cold harsh reality

This is a process
Each in their own way
Time may help
Time may not

Is that what death is
Losing pieces
Burying pieces
One at a time
Until sixth feet under
Where they are reunited whole

Glance

It is a picturesque sunset
As I comb the beach
Nothing but sounds are near me
Just miles of open sand

Waves crash upon the granules
As I feel the ocean's coolness
Like a lover's windblown kiss
I walk so carelessly

Though the appearance
Is designed to deceive
Really, I am lost
In a maze of emotions

I picture myself upon the sea
In a small boat rowing
Going in that direction
Accompanied by cold rough waters

I look for a lighthouse
But that beam of hope
Is nowhere in sight
I am battered about

Now I lose an oar
And the boat drifts
Without purpose
As do I

Losing seems to be a habit
That I am not able to be rid of
I take a mental picture
But smudges and blurriness taint it

My mind can be so kind
I look at what is there
Passed the black and white
Ignoring those hurtful words

If I tear the snapshot
What can I look upon
Maybe nothing
Maybe the solitary sea
Ever so vast
Yet empty
Like me

The Scarecrow

A crow flew down to me
And whispered into my ear
The crow was the messenger of death
The end of my existence was near

Fret or denial
Which choice to choose
In my paradox that is called life
Everything was at stake to lose

I captured the crow
Figuring if I had the avatar
Luck or pity would befall on me
Little did I know vengeance was the answer to be

Was it stupidity or madness
That got me chained to this scarecrow post
Death came to me in my sleep
And spoke of my childish boast

Now crows by the dozen come to my cornfield
Picking at my straw body
It is the punishment for defilement
It is the ending of a bittersweet love melody

The birds keep coming daily
Whispering sarcasms in my ears
"If only I had a brain"
They can be such sweet dears

Most of my straw interior
Now lies at my feet
I guess I have learned a lesson after all
Cheating death cannot be an accomplished feat

So as the wind blows more straw away
And the crows fly away for the winter
The mistress of death appears
In all of her malevolent splendor

Punishment was not her intention
On this introspective ride
It was a warning
That I was already dead inside

Lessons

The Sentinel

Since I was a little child
I knew I was different
A beacon for the weird
Abby Normal was standard

Horrific night terror unfolded
Intrusive whispering voices pleaded
Foreign thoughts and feelings haunted
Why am I the antennae

I am granted no peace
Being violated on a daily basis
Exposed and raw becomes the normal
Withdrawal and seclusion are a wishful vacation

A spirit guide comes
Offering solace and clarity
I take the opportune lifeline

And learn how to cope and deal

I discover this gift is not all bad
The good is out there
It is a matter of perspective
Even darkness has some light

This is not my happily ever after
But I have come to terms with what is
I do what I can
I am the witness, the sentinel

The Common Threads

The songs of early birds
Initiate the morning's concert
The orchestrated sunrise
Beams of intense light
Blaze over a lazy horizon
Through gathering clouds
Everything compared to this
Seems small and trivial

The young and old
Start to stir
From their warm slumber
Yawning and stretching
This turns into
Zombie-like movement
Both animal and man alike
Rises and aspires

The experienced old
Feed and advise the young
It is often
An underappreciated job
That receives little recognition
Nor praise
Nor thank you

The youthful offspring
Take selfishly
As their roles dictate
This is, of course
The survival of the fittest

For the one time each sunrise
Comes the unity of the planet
　　Best wishes to all
　　Let the day begin

The Storyteller

I leave the warmth of the bonfire
To make footprints in the sand
The ocean wants an audience
To listen to her poignant beauty

Worthless sand dollars bask
Sideway crabs zigzag
Frenzied sandpipers dash

Maniacal waves froth
Suicidal driftwood float
Stoic rocks wait

Majestic sandcastles stand
Aimless seaweed drift
Squawking seagulls glide

Cool wind whip
Splashing seals play
Pounding surf crash

Foggy clouds bellow
Moist sand squish
Salty sea air caress

Like always
She concludes her story with
The concert of the setting sun

The chapter ends
With lesson in hand
Knowing how small you are
But never alone

Philosophy

As I wander through life
Taking my analytical detailed notes
And aligning them with my morals
I try to approach each new situation
With both hands open
Though in the world today
I find myself reluctantly
With both fists closed
I do not desire combat
But when it happens
I unleash my inner warrior
Using love as my shield
And hate as my sword
The fighting is a violent spectacle
Sometimes a necessary evil
And when the dust settles
Or the last drop of blood falls
It is the truth that triumphs
For through all the victories
Or heart-wrenching defeats
It is you who will be found

Shadow of a Doubt

There is this strange person
To which I am often acquainted
Although our friendship is vague and estranged
He has always been there for me

He is a silent partner
In our unique relationship
His presence speaks volumes
But when we walk together
I am often noticed to be all alone

He has seen both sides
Of my Gemini madness
He expresses very little
Indifference is his specialty

I use him as a sounding board
To voice my hardships or concerns
Of course, he makes me work
For the possible solutions

I am very grateful to him
And give him credit for his wisdom
I see past his weakness
To the true person he will always be
Just a shadow

In the Eye of

If beauty is skin deep
Then your skin is made of glass
Oh dearest, please do forgive me
The truth is a torment all by itself

I do not wish to smash
That delicate vain self-image
Reflected in the carnival funhouse mirror
Which you base your beauty upon

I only want to glamourize
What I see in you
You do not need to hide behind
A cosmopolitan of advertising and flesh

Be honest with yourself my darling
On what you base as beauty
For when we look in the mirror
Do you even see the truth at all

Worth

What is your worth
Is it based on looks, brains, ability
Does doubt eat you up
Does hate wear you down

Do you know your passion
Do you have the heart to make it happen
Do you feel it in your bones
Do you have the grit to see it through

Listen to that inner voice, the positive one
Follow your moral compass, stay true
Take a long hard look, then improve
Fail, but get up again, and again

It is hard
It does suck
It hurts a lot
But follow your passion

Know your worth
Stand up, stand tall
Own it, show it
Inspire others to be like you

Hindsight

Sleep begins the possibilities of dreams
Some are exhilarating
Others are terrifying
The dreamer controls the dreamscape
But yet, that's with life in general too

Trial and error experiences in childhood
Help guide and mold the future aspirations
My question though is
How realistic should the dream be
Do I have the drive to really dream

Raw courage fuels the leap of faith
Into the past, into different dimensions, or into your soul
Because sometimes dreams are windows
With opportunities and deterrents across the sill
Even human arrogance and pride fog a clear view
Nevertheless, I still intently try

I build a dream, my dream
With concentric and concise precision
It is exactly what I want
It will be what I have dared for

At times, I fight for my dream
To keep the fire within the furnace blazing
Doubts challenge my happiness
One small prick and the dreams bleed
And could die

Then why is it
Anyone should aim to dream
With such obvious sorrow and pain abound
What good could come from this lunacy

I breathe in and focus
The answer is there
I take a baby step forward
With courage rising and daring

I unveil the truth
I embrace the bliss
I find myself
I dream

Baggage Claim

Why is it
When we move or vacation
That some baggage is never forgotten
Or better yet
Thrown out and left behind

The sight becomes palpable
To those curious lookiloos
Or for those brave few
Who dare to care

What has happened in the past
Has etched its scars
On our internal stone
Will you try to uncover
Or translate those damaged hieroglyphics
Do you become a baggage claim worker

Can you help relieve that questionable cargo
To ease a better voyage ahead
You know the load must be lightened
For the journey to continue

On the other hand
Stations are filled with lost damaged souls
Whose baggage has cost them more faire
Than they have investment

From past or present relationships
They reject help
Humility is not a strong point
Hope continues to die

Some fight fiercely for their luggage
For it is all they have
Half-truths and lies deny solid footing
As haunting whispers comforts anew

A heritage of abuse and pain
Becomes so interwoven
So imprisoning
The shackles birth a skewed reality
A weight demanded to be carried

Though hindered and hurt
The baggage remains
The journey loses momentum and direction
Energy and time are given to a different life
A cancerous future

So the question becomes
Though sins of the past have defined us
In the baggage that we labor to carry
Shouldn't we scrutinize said baggage
That governs our lives
And the freedom to be happy

The Box

It is dark in here
Even when my eyes adjust
Only to find
There is no way out

There are no doors
Nor windows
No furniture of any kind
It reminds me of a cell
But then that would make me
Its prisoner

I do not remember
How I happened to get here
Though now I ponder
How to get out
For I have been told
If you think long and hard enough
You will become the answer

I am reminded of Pandora
And her legacy with the Box
Evils were released
Apparently, curiosity did kill the cat
Or in this special case
Damned the whole world
But wait, I though Eve did that

Time stands still
As I experiment with possibilities
A newfound magic, my magic
Shapes a brave new world
The room is no longer empty
But then again
It never was

I create doors and windows
That will never open
I create loved ones
Without depth and warmth
It is something
It is better than nothing

If I feel trapped
I change the décor
It is easy enough
I will adjust
But Fate finds me
And calls me on my lie

My precious little world shatters
And to dark I must go
I roll up on the floor and cry
I wish for escape
I wish for change
Can I even try

It started as a soft whisper
Being followed by a spark of light
Speak the truth
Start anew
You are the answer

I blink my disbelieving eyes
I start to happy cry
I am the Jack out of the box
Before I scream elation
A haunting thought dares

Can I stay true
Will I do it again
It was so easy
To find that familiar dark path
And be back in the box

By Heart

I have led my life
Heart on my sleeve
I know that is dangerous
But it feels right

Sure, it hurts
Sometimes gets torn
If not downright bloody
But it is my way

If I am not real
Or honest or authentic
Then I am a lie, a sham
And that is not me

Raised to empathize
Walk in another's shoes
Cry when necessary
Hug when needed

A beating heart
Is such a wonderful thing
It leads like a band
Strong, bombastic, powerful

It drives you
It encapsulates life
It is the soul
So use it

The Masquerade

The gilded invitation arrives
Promising a very special night
I am finally recognized and included
Like a prince being crowned king by birthright

Such a grand formal affair
Demands I am dressed prim and proper
With no fairy godmother around
I must forgo being the pauper

I arrive at the castle in style
An immaculate phantom without the opera
Envious heads turn my way
My delighted smirk exposed by an envious candelabra

I descend the ostentatious staircase
Being greeted and accepted
I leave the last step, my past
Joining the upper echelon represented

Raucous laughter floats above the din
I absorb my good fortune then mirror
Luxury saunters and opulence shines
My eyes glint and crave that I have more

Hours have passed and midnight chimes
The crowd hushes as the facial facades fall
The truth of this wild night is revealed
There are no faces behind the masks at all

Hollow empty voids gaze about
The horror of what really is taunts and dares
I am rocked to my core and tremble
I turn away from those haunting stares

I run like Cinderella
Losing both glass slippers
I chose not to be like this, like them
Petty vacuous pretenders

I arrive home, tormented and exhausted
I look for a mirror, the moment of truth
I sigh with great relief and weep
There is a reflection

Mean Girls

It is another bad day
The judgments are flying
I try to be strong
I want to play along, play it off
But it is so hard
I feel alone

Shit, it is more than one person
I get it in high Dolby stereo
After a blink, it is a circle of them
I don't deserve this
No one does
Leave me alone

Now, the doubts in my head give voice
They add to the chorus of discourse
They taunt me
They cut me deep
They tear me down
I feel sadness, despair

I lose my courage
My self-image cracks
I run away
Tears burn my cheeks
As betrayal sets in
I hate feeling this weak

I find a corner and slump
Hoodie goes up
I withdraw
Seconds later, I get a tap
I uncover and look up
It is my teacher
Hunh

He smiles
He understands
"I see you"
"I like you"
"You're stronger than you know"
"You are a phoenix"

I give one last sniffle and nod
I am not alone
Now, I smirk
I take back my power
I stand
No, I rise

Everyday Princess

There are those "people"
When you notice them
For the first time
You say, "Wow, who is that"
It is that notable

It is a beauty and grace
That knows no limits
It is a kindness and vulnerability
That draws you in
Magnetic doesn't even cover it

You have heard the tales
With its woes and hardships
Courage and grit
See her through
Set her free

Does she know her power
Of what she can do
No fairy godmother was needed
She did it all on her own
Belief and passion were enough

It is a wonder to behold
Though it is a quiet shine
Rare and valuable
I guess that is why
She is an everyday princess

By Heart

I have led my life
Heart on my sleeve
I know that is dangerous
But it feels right

Sure, it hurts
Sometimes gets torn
If not downright bloody
But it is my way

If I am not real
Or honest or authentic
Then I am a lie, a sham
And that is not me

Raised to empathize
Walk in another's shoes
Cry when necessary
Hug when needed

A beating heart
Is such a wonderful thing
It leads like a band
Strong, bombastic, powerful

It drives you
It encapsulates life
It is the soul
So use it

Happening Now

I am tired of the naysayers, the haters
Trying to keep me down
Shutting me out
Too bad, so sad
This isn't about you
This is all on me, about me
Head held high
Eyes on the prize
Soon, they will know my name

I am a believer
Strong and resilient
This is about my future
I won't stop
This is who I am
Determined and audacious
Just wait and see

I may stumble
I may fall
That is what grit is for
It is what faith is about
I rise
I fight
I try even harder
It is about a mindset
Watch me go
Succeed, lead

This is my mission
It is not about some day
It will happen
I swear
One day
Real soon

Full Circle

When I get angry or hurt
I contemplate, then write
I wreaking-ball the dam
Letting the "good" times flow

This process is cathartic
Wisdom has shown me that
I get the emotional poison out
I exorcise the negativity
I do not want this to be a part of me

It is all about
How I handle the situation
That is on me
My words, my actions
That is of my making

I own that
Right or wrong
Good and ugly
I am not perfect
No one is

I revisit the past
Ignoring the judgments
Critiquing both sides
Learning from the experience

Know the history
Walk in their shoes
Empathize
Understand
Forgive

Exposed

When I strike the last computer key
The struggle is over
I sit back in awe and wonder
I have created new life

If you are an author
Then you understand what I mean
The hard part comes next
Letting it go, letting it be seen

It is nerve racking
The beta readers, the editors
Will they get it, like it
I now wait, (you have to)

Time becomes the enemy
Idle hands and all
Nagging doubts resurface
The silence is quite deafening

Your baby finally comes back
Blood drawn, inoculated
You rock it
Loving it again

You sigh with relief
A hopeful proud parent
You edit and polish
Getting ready for the send off

You finish
It is ready, it is time
Time to let it go
Forever

Teachable Moments

I get great pleasure
When I see
One of my students
Know it, get it

The surprise exhilarates
The realization wows
The ownership lifts
The pride beams

Yes, that was all you
It was there all along
You did it
Now, you can see it

When that door of belief opens
A new world of possibilities arrives
It is tangible
It is doable

Today, I made an impact
A badge of honor to behold
A moment to remember
Sometimes, that is all you need

Funny-ish

You Don't Know Jack

Jack be clumsy
Jack be slow
Jack wanted success
Like a famous star on a TV show

If he did that
Then he would be a fat cat
Jack dashed off on his run
"Boy, this will be such fun"

Unfortunately, Jack tripped and fumbled
All coolness gone, leaving only a grumble
Into a deep abandoned well he fell
He screamed, "What the bloody hell?"

Jack hit the bottom
With a loud grunt and a thump
Good thing it was
On his royal plump rump

"Gosh almighty
What a huge mess
Boy, Mom will be mad
That I dirtied and tore my best dress"

Jack looked up
And started to wail and cry
Numerous tears flowed
From Jack's one good eye

Deep trouble
Jack became
For you see
This well had no drain

Water filled
Over Jack's head
Jack could not swim
So Jack became dead

What is the moral
Of this awful tragic story
Be happy with who you are
Nothing is worth that kind of glory

Mean Coach Mike

The bell has rung
The whistle has rattled
The time is up
Now comes the battle

Children, recess is over
Just go to class
Please children go
I order you alas

Go to class children
With no more talk
Listen children listen
Walk, walk, walk

But Coach Mike
We want to stay and play
Whether rain or shine
All hours of the day

Coach Mike replies
Children, I do not think so
The rules do not change
Please children go

The children do not go
They plead away to stay
Some try to hug him
To get him to sway

Please Coach Mike
The teachers won't care
Just a little more time
Answer our innocent prayer

Coach Mike is a rock
No children no
You must go to class
To learn and to grow

No more building sand castles
No more trips down the slide
No more monkeying on the bars
It is time to go inside

No more kicking the soccer ball
No more hitting the tetherballs
No more jumping rope
It is time to walk in the halls

No more drinks at the fountains
No more visits to the bathrooms
No more trips to the office
Please children go to your classrooms

You sure are mean
The children do say
Not nice at all
Not any ole day

Mean Coach Mike gets serious
I am sorry to ruin your fun
My job is order and safety
A most difficult one

It is full of speeding tickets
And green and red cards
It is full of naughty children on the wall
It is really quite hard

I do not like doing mean things
But I do what I must
Children must be orderly and safe
It is an extension of a parent's trust

So please children go
Your playtime is up
Off to your classrooms
With a big giddy-up

Coach Mike said go
And go is what he meant
The children accepted the truth
So the saddened children finally went

What a relief for Coach Mike
That this battle is won
Though he is still considered mean
By most every young one

The children march off to class
In their quiet orderly lines
It is a job well done
But what will happen the next recess time

Kyle Wouldn't Mind, So Out He Went

From day one
Mrs. Storm said
Behave young ones
Before I become red

I will be so mad
You wouldn't want to know
I will give you the boot
And out you will go

I will call Coach Mike
And he will toss you on the roof
To that mean ole scary troll
With yellow teeth, sharp horns, and a broken hoof

The troll will chain you up
In its rooftop of horrors
No one can hear you scream
Or save you from its nasty horrors

The troll beats you with wet sticky noodles
Or throws live earthworm mud pies
You are hit with messy wiggling splats
Right between your scared bulging eyes

The troll feeds you broccoli and grasshopper soup
With cauliflower and moth salad
But watch out for the sewer water Perrier
It is really quite torrid and putrid

So one day, Kyle did not mind
He did not even care
That old Mrs. Storm is just bluffing
To give us a frightful old scare

On that day, Kyle did not listen
Mrs. Storm threw him out
Coach Mike was called
And took Kyle about

Up on the roof
Kyle did fly
A big satisfying thud was echoed
But Kyle did not even cry

When Kyle stood up
The mean old scary troll did appear
Just like Mrs. Storm said
Now Kyle shed a tear

Instantly, Kyle pleaded and promised
That he will be really good
Desperately, he hoped and prayed
That the mean ole scary troll understood

Menacingly, the troll clomped to Kyle
And whispered in his trembling ear
I have your word on this
But remember, I am very near

Quickly, Kyle nodded
But the situation was far from over
Kyle was still on the roof
With a troll who likes to closely hover

By its sharp horns
The troll picked up poor Kyle
And tossed him off the roof
With such enthusiastic guile

Kyle crashed into the bushes below
Mostly, safe and sound
He did have a leaf here or there
But at least, he was back on the ground

Kyle scrambled out of the bushes
And bolted back to class
He said he was very sorry
And warned the class alas

It is all true
What Mrs. Storm said
You have to be very good
Or you will be filled with such horrible dread

So for the rest of the year
The children did what they were told
Especially, that spunky little Kyle
Because he did not want to again meet that scary ole troll

Reality

When I woke this morning
I felt light-headed
Cotton mouth tasting nasty
Guess the alcohol was still embedded

What was I thinking last night
Being the drunken fool
All that bumping and grinding
What a fucking tool

I fall out of bed
And crawl to the bathroom
The light burns brightly
Until I turn it back to gloom

Feeling dizzy and nauseous
I comprehend the reality with a nod
A gross burp starts it all
The offering to the porcelain god

I barely move an inch
When my joints and head begin to ache
Why did I even bother
To even become awake

A Simple Wish

The lights are dimmed
When this all starts
Loved ones surround you
Connected together like puzzle parts

Conversations whisper and die
When the match is struck
Candle after candle is lit
It is a measure of good luck

Thoughts turn to wishes
That bubble and burst
What a churning sensation
Did you pick the third wish or the first

Suddenly, a deep breath is taken
And your lips become pursed
It is a moment of triumph
It seems so many times rehearsed

A gentle blown kiss
Whips the dancing flames about
One by one their burning passions flicker
And begrudgingly wink out

When you blow out the candles
On your fancy birthday cake
Do you ever wonder what happens
To all those wishes that you make

They rise with the smoke
Transmuting into phoenix-like hope
It is warm fuzzies abound
From those who love you, you big dumb loveable dope

Happy Birthday!

Vino

It is amazing to think
That a small round fruit
Can become such
A transformative medium

It comes in many colors
In many wonderful flavors
Peppery and spicy
Aged and smooth

To each their own
By the glass or by the bottle
Clink and satiate the palette
It is a festive occasion every time

When married to the right food
The flavors are enhanced
What an incredible rush
It is almost orgasmic

So invite some loved ones
Pop a cork or two
Sniff, swirl, and serve
Savoring the generosity abound

Salud

Books

They sit on a shelf and wait
They lounge on a bedside table
There is adventure, mystery, and horror abound
All it takes is time and courage

Pick me up
Caress my spine
Spread me wide open
Oops, did I forget romance

Tickle your fancy
Settle in a comfy chair
Jump right on in
It is always better than a movie

You get sucked in
Time stands still
You get taken away
Isn't it nice to be fulfilled

Thank You

We often don't say
Thank you enough
So thank you
For supporting me
It is
Highly, truly
Appreciated

Made in the USA
Monee, IL
18 January 2024